How to Massage Your Dog

by
Jane Buckle

Illustrations by Ron Young

HOWELL
BOOK
HOUSE

For my friend Nettie.

Howell Book House
MACMILLAN
A Simon & Schuster Macmillan Company
1633 Broadway
New York, NY 10019

Library of Congress Cataloging-in-Publication Data

Buckle, Jane.
    How to massage your dog/Jane Buckle.
       p.   cm.
    ISBN 0-87605-645-1
    1. Dogs--Diseases--Alternative treatment. 2. Massage
    for animals
    I. Title.
    SF991.B83   1995
    636.089'5822--dc20   95-16893
                                 CIP

Manufactured in the United States of America
10 9 8 7 6 5 4 3 2

Contents

Introduction

This book was written to fulfill the needs of dogs and their owners. Dog owners want to make their pets feel good. They also want to feel good about themselves. Following years of practicing massage and aromatherapy on humans, I began to think it could be the turn of our four-footed friends.

During one Christmas vacation, while casually massaging a fearsome-looking Rottweiler, my friend asked me what I was doing to her dog. Realizing that petting her dog had actually turned into a massage, I replied, *I am massaging Nora.* My friend raised an eyebrow, smiled and asked, *Oh, how do you massage a dog?*

This book was born.

Principles

Chapter 1

Why Massage Your Dog?

Just like human beings, pets adore being cared for. Massage is a natural way to increase the bond between you and your dog. Massage is actually good for your dog, too. It increases blood circulation, helps aches and pains, reduces blood pressure, soothes away fears, and encourages relaxation.

The sort of massage you will want to give your dog is slow and gentle. The proper name for the strokes you will be using is *effleurage,* which means stroking in French; France is where this massage technique comes from.

Ensure that you are comfortably dressed before you begin.

By indulging in a little tactile pleasure, you will strengthen the relationship and trust between you and your pet, and you will improve your health.

Chapter 2

When to Massage Your Dog

It is a good idea to try to establish some kind of special time so your pet will know when his moment has come and eventually might draw your attention to it by bringing you his massage mat or towel.*

Don't worry if you find it difficult to establish a routine immediately. You will need time to discover which kind of massage you enjoy giving the most.

Some insomniacs find nighttime perfect for giving their dog a massage. Indeed, research shows that massage is very therapeutic for insomniacs.

As you may both end up falling asleep together, choose a place you will find comfortable to wake up in.

A word on massage mats. These can be made very inexpensively by covering a piece of foam with a dog-appreciable fabric, like a bone pattern.

Chapter 3

Where to Massage Your Dog

Choose a place where you are unlikely to be interrupted, preferably somewhere warm, with no drafts. Dim the lights: Your pet will find it difficult to relax with a spotlight on him. Switch on the answering machine and pin a note to your front door saying, *Back in half an hour.*

Bedrooms can be perfect places for a dog massage — especially if they are usually off-limits. By choosing a room not normally available to your pet, he will soon get the idea that when you both go there he is going to receive some great massage therapy.

Chapter 4

How Often to Massage Your Dog

Start off with once a week, and build up from there until a massage becomes part of your daily routine. As time goes on and you become more expert, you will look forward to these moments of intimacy more and more.

Never think of massage as a chore. It is one of the greatest gifts you can give your pet. It is free, it is good for you, it is good for him, and it should be nonaddictive. Do not be surprised if you experience a little family jealousy, however.

If this happens, indulge in a family massage from time to time.

Chapter 5

Massage Mediums

What do you use to massage your dog? Well, hands are fine by themselves, but if you would like to make your pet's coat glossier and improve his skin, use a little cold-pressed vegetable oil. Grapeseed oil, sweet almond oil, or the fabulous Jojoba oil are ones you could try. *Do not use cooking oil.* Cooking oils are only meant for cooking.

The best sort of oils for a massage can usually be purchased in a health food shop and are often labeled "for massage." Do not use prepared aromatherapy oils, as these could cause an allergic or sensitive reaction in your pet. *Do not use bath oils.*

Use the oil very sparingly, and, over the months, you will see your pet's coat become glossy and thick.

Chapter 6

Massage Technique I: Palm Strokes

Hold the flat part of your hand in a slightly cupped position, palm facing downwards. Then, with both hands, gently massage your pet, using a breast-stroke-like motion with both palms working in tandem.

As you push away from yourself, make the stroke heavier; then keep the returning stroke toward you very light. It is the difference in pressure that adds to the relaxation, and pleasure, of a massage.

This technique works well on large areas of your pet. Make sure you keep your shoulders nice and relaxed. Think of South Sea islands, gentle breezes, and palm trees.

Chapter 7

Massage Technique II: Thumb Strokes

Draw tiny circles with your thumbs, using both simultaneously. Don't make the pressure too light. Use slow, circular movements to produce a delicious, tingly sensation.

Do not use this technique directly on the spine, which would be painful, but on each side, which feels lovely. Try this out on a friend (a good friend!) first to get some feedback.

Of all the massage strokes, this is the one that is often voted the favorite. Close your eyes for a moment and feel the tissues and muscles of your pet underneath your thumbs. Feel tissue and muscle slowly relax as tension and aches are soothed away. Lean forward gently, allowing some of your body weight to pass into your thumbs.

This technique puts a whole new meaning into the song, "Thumbelina"!

Chapter 8

Massage Technique III: "Fish" Strokes

Hold your hands up as though they are fishes' mouths opening and closing. Watch and feel how you make these movements. You are going to do the same thing but with your hands horizontal, not vertical. This will knead the skin of your pet between your fingers and thumbs as you open and close the fishes' mouths.

Use first one hand, then the other hand, alternatively, letting the fish-mouths swim toward each other. Work diagonally, using a rhythmic pattern and criss-crossing. This is an extremely soothing massage and can be used on most areas of your pet. Apply more pressure on the hind quarters and less on the abdomen.

Keep the rhythm slow. You are an angel fish, not a piranha!

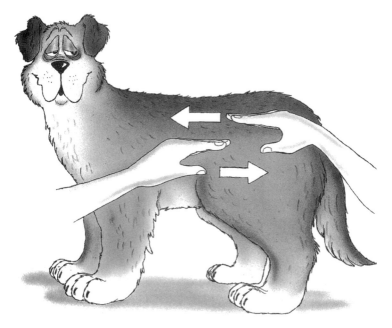

Parts
of the Body

Chapter 9

Head and Face Massage

This massage can produce a smile or a snarl, and is best practiced on yourself in the mirror first until you get the hang of moving both hands simultaneously in a non-jerky motion.

Tell your dog what you are going to do, and hopefully he will close his eyes. Remember to use very gentle, small circles. Avoid the eye orbit, nose, and inside the ears. Concentrate on your dog's jowls, forehead, back of head, and neck.

When you are practiced in this, if you listen carefully you may hear your dog sigh with pleasure. Candlelight can enhance these magic moments.

Chapter 10

Slow Back Massage

Most dogs adore having their backs massaged, and it is often the most acceptable place to begin.

Start gently, very slowly, making circles with your thumbs on each side of the spine, using the thumb massage technique. You will feel the bony outline of the spine very clearly. With small circular movements, slowly work your way down each side of the spine, moving your thumbs simultaneously. Do this three times.

Then follow with three lots of slow palm strokes, then three lots of slow fish strokes, before beginning again with the thumb strokes. Continue this regime until your pet becomes sleepy or rolls over.

Chapter 11

Fast Back Massage

This is to energize your dog, not to make him feel sleepy, so the movements should be rapid and brisk. Use the same regime as in the slow back massage, just do it faster.

By the end of the session, your face should be red and glowing, and the coat of your pet should be standing up. You will both be ready for some vigorous exercise, like a 10-mile hike.

This is a great massage for chasing the blues away, clearing your mind, and working off some of that extra helping of apple pie.

Chapter 12

Chest Massage

This can easily be done following a head and face, or a back massage. Encourage your pet to roll onto her back. Once she is lying happily, paws upward, begin massaging the chest area in small, circular movements, using the thumb massage technique.

Remember to keep the pressure fairly light, but do not tickle. Move in a large, square formation, and don't forget to pay attention to the "armpit" areas. Fish and palm strokes don't work so well. Keep the movements slow and even.

If you have problems delineating between chest and stomach, do not attempt after feeding.

Chapter 13

Front Paw and Leg Massage

It is usually a good idea to hold your pet's paw quietly for a moment before you begin this type of massage, so he will get the idea that this is going to be fun. It will also give you a clear indication if he is going to allow you to do it at all.

Front paws are easier to massage than back paws because your pet can sit down and watch. Use thumb strokes, and *please be gentle.* Work only on the top of the paw, not the pad underneath. When you have finished one paw, move over to the other before starting on the legs.

Then work your way up and down each leg using fish strokes. Massage each leg for at least five minutes. This is especially good for elderly dogs.

Chapter 14

Back Paw and Leg Massage

The back legs of elderly dogs can become very arthritic. Massage is a wonderful way to soothe the pain and encourage better blood flow. Naturally, if your pet has aches and pains, he will be wary until he knows how good the massage feels.

Holding a dog by one of his hind legs can feel threatening, as it sets him off balance. When you do this massage, encourage him to lean against either you or a piece of furniture until he feels confident he won't fall over. Talking to him will give reassurance.

He may insist on sitting down, which will make the massage more difficult. The best position for you, then, is a sitting one with him between your legs. If he is a very large dog, this can pose problems.

Chapter 15

Tail Massage

This is a wonderful massage if your dog has a long tail or, actually, any tail. However, if your dog has a very short tail or no tail, it can be a problem. If this is the case, move your hands slowly in the area of a phantom tail and watch your pet's face very carefully. When you have ascertained the correct phantom outline, your pet will begin to smile.

For those of you who have pets with long tails, remember to massage the entire length of the tail. Always work toward the end of the tail, not toward the body. Your pet will treat this massage as a great game, and you can both spend hours of fun chasing his tail until you collapse with exhaustion. Your pet will particularly appreciate your sense of play and the resurrection of his puppyhood.

Chapter 16
No-Go Areas of Your Dog

It is important to understand there are some parts of a dog that are better not massaged. Bear in mind that your dog could be embarrassed at the sudden display of affection you are giving him and, therefore, may be more sensitive — especially in certain spots.

Definite no-go areas are those in which you would rather not be licked yourself, particularly by your dog. If you do go over the boundaries, be assured your dog will tell you.

Types of Dogs

Chapter 17

Massage for Puppies

The best way to ensure your dog will grow up liking massage is to start massaging him in his puppyhood. All good dog mothers lick their babies during puppyhood; massage is a natural extension of this.

Always explain what you want to do to the mother and ask her permission first.

Puppies are rarely still for long, and massaging one can be an art. However, do not be put off. With a little perseverance, your puppy will get the message (and the massage!). By watching you massage his brothers or sisters, your puppy will know what to expect when his turn comes.

Then, the only problem will be how many puppies can you massage at the same time? With a little practice, and using your feet, you could handle four.

Chapter 18

Massage for Elderly Dogs

Just like us, animals become stiff in their joints as they get older. They are less keen to run after a ball, or to run at all. Gradual loss of the use of their hind legs means circulation to their kidneys is reduced. This can have serious effects. One way to help your pet is to massage her hindquarters.

Begin gently, with circular movements, using both thumbs. You will feel your pet's stiff, tense muscles. Be sensitive, and only begin to press a little deeper as she, and her muscles, begin to relax. Follow with fish strokes. Not only will you be helping her joints, but you will also be helping her circulation, and that can help allay kidney problems.

A little classical music will help — Mozart is excellent for elderly dogs.

Chapter 19

Massage for Hyperactive Dogs

Hyperactive dogs can be exhausting to own. They never sit still, bark at the slightest noise (imagined or not), and have a bottomless supply of energy. However, these highly strung, supersensitive animals will readily respond to this one-on-one therapy.

Use a combination of strokes on all parts of this dog's body. By developing a regular schedule you will be able to repeat the exact combination at the same time each day. Hyperactive animals like familiarity and will grow more peaceful with each session — and so will you!

Keep your voice soft and quiet and tell your dog over and over and over that everything is going to be just fine; by the end of the session you will both believe it — and it will probably be true.

Chapter 20

Massage for Pregnant Dogs

Dogs, like humans, appreciate extra tenderness when they are pregnant. Because they are carrying extra weight, they are more prone to aches and pains, particularly backaches.

Massage on pregnant pets is best carried out with them lying on their side. A small cushion under your pet's head will ensure real comfort.

Massage very lightly from the spine around toward the stomach area. Use fish strokes and keep them light, smooth, and slow. Do not be put off if the puppies decide to play basketball during the massage — they are merely showing their appreciation and getting some insider training!

Chapter 21

Massage for Couch Potatoes

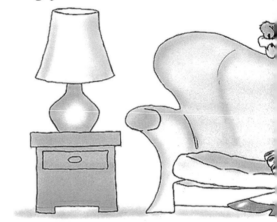

Some dogs become bored with play and end up watching TV all day while munching dog biscuits. These dogs need stimulation. An invigorating massage will help break the couch-potato syndrome.

First of all, turn off the TV. Put on some Latin American dance music and begin to massage your

pet with your hands, allowing your body to move freely in time to the music. (Experienced masseurs always use their bodies — it is much less tiring.)

Do not be surprised if your pet begins to sway in time to the music. Over a period of weeks you can progress to the tango.

But make sure you lead.

Chapter 22

Massage for Skeptical Dogs

We all know these types of dogs — they are the ones who take ages to try out a new food and refuse to go a different way around the block. Gentleness is the key to winning them over, as is a sense of fun.

Try wearing a clip-on red nose or a revolving bow-tie. Skeptical dogs always have a keen sense of humor.

It may take a couple of weeks to gain this one's confidence and interest, but *all* dogs will eventually allow you to turn a pat into a massage.

Chapter 23

Massage for Purebreds

Purebreds need careful handling; they know they are special. Always use your pet's full name (the very long one on his registration certificate) and keep repeating it like a mantra throughout the massage. This will confirm your pet's pedigree to him and reassure him you respect his identity.

Always finish the massage with a handshake.

Chapter 24

Massage for Uninterested Dogs

Never underestimate the disdain of an uninterested dog. A back can be a very expressive thing. Given a gentle loving massage, however, your dog's look of disdain will very soon become, "If I sit like this will you massage me, please?"

When this happens, don't be tempted to show your disinterest!

Chapter 25

Massage for Tiny Dogs

Be very gentle with tiny dogs. Toy Poodles are called that for a reason — they are delicate and can be damaged with rough play. Keep your strokes firm but fairly soft. Remember, your pet is flesh and blood. How would you like King Kong to massage you?

Do not tickle. That is worse. Dogs may have a great sense of humor, but have you actually ever heard one laugh?

Chapter 26

Massage for Huge Dogs

Apart from taking up a lot of oil, it doesn't matter how large your dog is, he will still benefit from receiving a massage.

Just like humans, the larger the animal, the more likely he is to suffer from joint aches and pains. Large dogs take more time, so adjust your schedule so you do not need to hurry.

Be wary of being rolled on by your pet when he has reached a state of bliss.

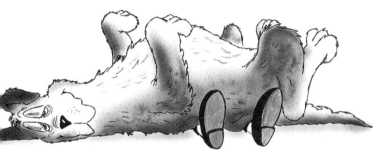

Chapter 27

Massage for City Dogs

City dogs are used to being left at home, sometimes all day, while their owners go to work. These
dogs can suffer from depression and eating disor-
ders as a result of feeling temporarily abandoned.

A regular evening massage for your animal,
when you return home, is the perfect accompani-
ment to your usual gin and tonic. It allows mutual
bonding and will relax both you and your pet.

It can also set the scene for a romantic dinner
à deux. Make sure it is you who sets the table.

Chapter 28

Massage for Country Dogs

Country dogs are not used to being pampered. They may not understand massages at all, to begin with. Massaging them could also cause a few problems with the other animals around the homestead, who may also want this special treatment.

The best way to deal with letting everyone in on the action is to firmly carry out the first massage, then post a notice on the barn door stating that all animals will be massaged in strict order of first come, first served, with the time and date.

Be prepared for a rush.

51

Chapter 29

Massage for Jealous Dogs

Dogs can get jealous of a new friend, new partner, or new baby. One way to help them is to make them feel as loved and secure as possible. Indulge them in a small massage whenever possible, especially when the new friend, partner, or baby is in the room. Even a couple of minutes will do.

This is a very special way of ensuring that your pet gets the attention he craves. By gradually associating the new person with a good experience, your pet will understand he does not need to come between you and the other loved ones in your life.

Chapter 30

Massage for Adopted Dogs

Rescued dogs, or those adopted from shelters or pounds, are especially vulnerable. Often they have been the victims of abandonment, mistreatment, and other cruelties.

They will need a great deal of tender loving care to put all those memories behind them.

It may take a little while to relieve their fears of touch, and change their expectation of abuse into anticipation of pleasure. A regular bedtime massage will help.

Remember to tuck them in with their favorite blanket and toy.

Chapter 31

Massage for Convalescing Dogs

We all know how boring convalescing is, especially for the once-active. Having to put up with a leg in plaster is all the more irritating if interesting smells and sounds have to be ignored.

Gentle massage will help your pet to relax, encourage circulation, and guard against stiff muscles — but keep the massage strokes well away from the injured site. Encourage lots of fluid intake and keep your pet warm.

A get-well card is always appreciated.

Beyond the Basics

Chapter 32

Massage by Disabled Owners

Disabled owners have a great advantage — they are usually on hand to give a massage, and they often turn out to be the most skilled. No matter if you are in a wheelchair, are bedridden, or are partially sighted, your pet will really appreciate the skill and love a massage will give her.

Small pets can be easily accommodated on your lap. Larger pets will happily stand, sit still, or lie on your bed beside you while you carry out your magic.

Research shows that giving a pet a massage will greatly benefit you, too.

Chapter 33

Massage by Children

When you teach your children how to care for the family pet, both pet and children benefit. Massage can be a part of this care.

Be sure to supervise the sessions until both parties are confident of themselves — and each other. Even very young children can help.

But do be wary of identity problems!

Chapter 34

Massage by Teenagers

Teenagers cannot do anything without music, usually very loud music. This is fine provided you can find a spare set of headphones for your pet that are not connected to the boom box. They will protect him against the volume, but at the same time will allow him to feel included (remember, dogs have ultrasensitive ears).

Your teenager will bop away with the music and will find massaging the family pet a real cinch. Your pet will be safely ensconced behind soundproof headphones and will enjoy a really contemporary connection with the next generation, without being deafened in the process.

Chapter 35

Massage as Part of Training

By incorporating massage into your set schedule of obedience training, your pet will avoid the risk of being overindulged in the more traditional cheese or dog biscuit rewards.

When your pet begins to understand that massage could be the chosen reward, you can begin to ask her preference.

Remember to allow time for this in your personal planner. You could code it DM (for Dog Massage), which looks sufficiently like Deputy Manager or Direct Mail not to cause embarrassment.

REWARDS
TREATS
TOYS
MASSAGE ✓

Chapter 36

Massage by Foot

Anyone who has ever experienced a Thai massage knows just how delicious a foot massage feels. Just slip off your shoes and socks and indulge in a little toe wriggling up and down your dog's back. He will reciprocate and, together, you can indulge in some happy mutual wriggling.

This is best attempted after a large Sunday lunch, preferably while watching the Big Game on the tube.

Make sure your toenails are short.

Chapter 37

Four-Handed Massage

For the ultimate in bliss, ask another member of the family to massage your pet with you. This will give your pet a double dose of loving touch.

It is usually not a good idea to ask the cat....

Chapter 38

Massage on Thanksgiving and Other Holidays

It is all too easy in the hustle and bustle of preparing for holiday festivities to become engrossed in family business and not leave enough time for your pet.

But never forget that your dog is your best friend.

Letters . . .

Chapter 39

Letters from Satisfied Dogs

From Caesar, a grateful Lab:

I am so pleased you practiced on me, Jane Buckle. Now my mistress and master massage me often. I know they have loved and cared for me for many years, but sometimes, in my advancing years, when they have patted me, it has hurt. Now they massage me gently, and the effect on my stiff old hindquarters has been wonderful. My joints have not ached nearly so much, and I look forward to the twice-weekly sessions in the pool room. Thank you.

From Mandy, the Mutt:

I was a little skeptical when you started touching me in this new manner, but I must admit it is very relaxing and does help take my mind off our regular trips to the veterinarian. I especially like the oil, which smells slightly nutty. With many woofs of pleasure. Yours faithfully.

From Emma, the West Highland White Terrier:

A few weeks ago I ran after the neighbor's cat and slipped, causing me to limp afterwards. At first my owner tried to help by letting me rest, but we terriers aren't very good at resting, are we? Well, the wonderful massages she gave me after reading your book not only relaxed the hurt muscles but helped me rest and heal. Just wait until I see that cat again!

From Cleo, the Basset Hound:

I am so glad you wrote this book. Speaking for my fellow dogs, we could all use this. Thank you, and much wagging of the tail now that I can finally sleep through the night.

From William, the Briard:

I know I am a big boy, but I am a softie at heart and really loved the massage my master learned from your book. It helped bring my blood pressure down. Thank you, and when's the next one coming out?

P.S. I'd like to send this as a gift to everyone we know.

Chapter 40

Letters from Satisfied Owners

Dear Jane,

Thank you so much for your book. I bought it for my husband for his birthday, but everyone in the family managed to read it in one day! We all laughed so much. But you know, it really works! We didn't think it would, but our dog, Maldoon, who is normally hyperactive, has been so relaxed after his session. We keep looking at him to see if he is the same dog! Thank you.

The Bristol Family

Dear Jane,

My ancient Collie, Meg, has been my best friend for 15 years. Now in the twilight of her life, she has obvious pain in her back legs. My daughter gave me your book last week. I thought I would try to massage Meg, although I was very nervous. But Meg kept licking my hands when I stopped, so I carried on massaging her for a full half-hour. Her walking is so much more supple now! Thank you. It is wonderful to be able to help her.

Mrs. K.S.

Dear Jane,

I bought your book for my aunt, but after I began reading it I decided I just had to keep it, it was so funny. I don't have a dog, but I can't wait to try out some of the strokes on my aunt's dog — only then will I let her see where I learned them!

Tracey M.

Dear Jane,

Your book is not just funny, it is informative and much needed. If only people would massage their dogs when they felt stressed, they wouldn't need to come and clutter up my waiting room.

A Psychiatrist

Dear Jane,

At long last a funny book that actually teaches dog owners how to improve their pet care. Well done. Perhaps we veterinarians should all buy two copies — one to keep ourselves, and one to leave in the waiting room.

A Veterinarian

... And Your Just Reward

If you have followed along with all the techniques discussed and illustrated in this book, your dog should be a very happy, contented, fit and above all, much-loved pet indeed!

And if your dog loves you as much in return, and is as smart as you believe, perhaps you will receive a wonderful reward — a gentle paw massage to your back!

You never know your luck.